S0-AAD-798

FORTNITE:
Combat

CHERRY LAKE PUBLISHING • ANN ARBOR, MICHIGAN

by Josh Gregory

Published in the United States of America by Cherry Lake Publishing
Ann Arbor, Michigan
www.cherrylakepublishing.com

Reading Adviser: Marla Conn MS, Ed., Literacy specialist, Read-Ability, Inc.

Library of Congress Cataloging-in-Publication Data
Names: Gregory, Josh, author.
Title: Fortnite. Combat / by Josh Gregory.
Other titles: Combat
Description: Ann Arbor, Michigan : Cherry Lake Publishing, 2019. | Series:
  Unofficial guides | Series: 21st century skills innovation library |
  Includes bibliographical references and index. | Audience: Grade 4 to 6.
Identifiers: LCCN 2019003339 | ISBN 9781534148130 (lib. bdg.) |
  ISBN 9781534150997 (pbk.) | ISBN 9781534149564 (pdf) |
  ISBN 9781534152427 (ebook)
Subjects: LCSH: Fortnite (Video game)—Juvenile literature.
Classification: LCC GV1469.35.F67 G744 2019 | DDC 294.8—dc23
LC record available at https://lccn.loc.gov/2019003339

Cherry Lake Publishing would like to acknowledge the work of the Partnership for
21st Century Learning. Please visit www.p21.org for more information.

Printed in the United States of America
Corporate Graphics

Contents

Chapter 1

Action Packed

t's no secret that *Fortnite* has taken the world by storm. This incredibly thrilling video game combines fast-paced shooting action with strategic building to create an experience that is

Fortnite is the type of game where you might find yourself zip-lining up the side of a mountain while dressed as a very strong Santa Claus.

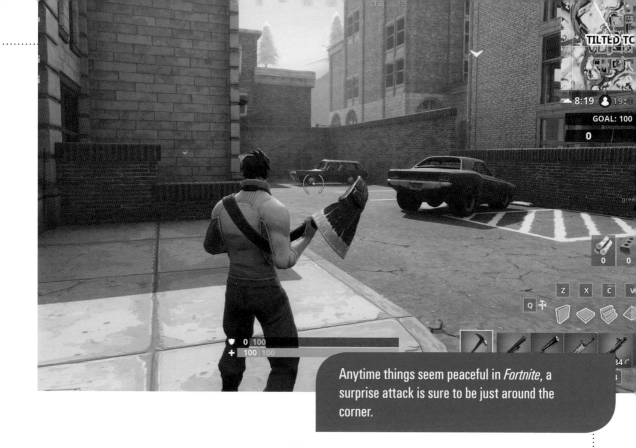

Anytime things seem peaceful in *Fortnite*, a surprise attack is sure to be just around the corner.

unlike anything else. Sometimes it seems like everyone is playing the game. This means you have to be really good if you want to stand out!

When you jump into your first *Fortnite* match, things might seem quiet and calm. There might not be any other players nearby. But once the action starts, you'll find that everything happens very fast in this game. Rival players will launch attacks from all sides. Rockets and grenades will explode all around you. Giant towers, walls, and ramps seem to appear out of nowhere. You might even spot an enemy speeding toward you in a dangerous-looking vehicle.

If you don't avoid all of these dangers, your character can be knocked out of the match in almost no time at all. And even as you're defending yourself, you also need to think about fighting back if you want to win. All of this action can be a lot for new players to keep track of.

If you find a vehicle, you can zoom around the island much faster than you can get around on foot.

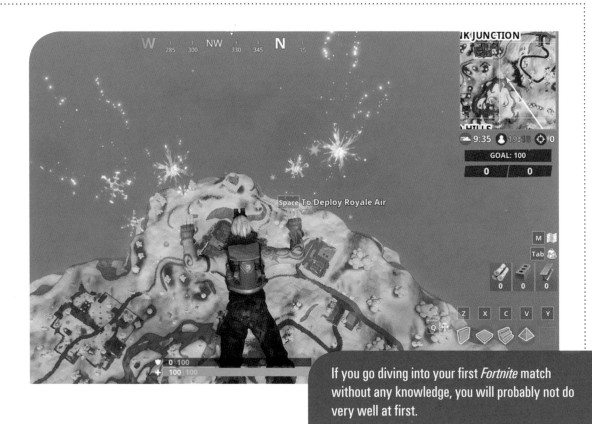

If you go diving into your first *Fortnite* match without any knowledge, you will probably not do very well at first.

When you watch friends or **streamers** play *Fortnite*, you might wonder how they got so good. They move incredibly fast, aim their weapons perfectly, and can build complicated structures without even thinking about it. Everything they do in the game seems as natural to them as walking or talking. How did they get to be so great at *Fortnite*?

Succeeding at *Fortnite* combat requires knowledge, skill, and reflexes. You need to know a lot about the game, from how different weapons work to how major landmarks are arranged on the map. You will also need to know when and how to build different structures and which combat strategies work best in different situations. Finally, you simply need to be able to think and move quickly. You'll need to make important decisions in a split second.

Playing alongside other people online can help you last longer in Battle Royale matches.

Teaming Up

One of the most fun things about *Fortnite* is that you can join up with your friends and play together online. If you are new to the game, playing on a team with a more experienced friend can be a great way to learn new skills. Your friend can show you the ropes and help protect you from attacks. If your character gets knocked down, your teammates can even **revive** you.

If you don't have any friends who play *Fortnite*, you can still team up with other players. If you are in either the Duos or Squads mode, you will see an option to switch between "fill" and "don't fill" on the lobby screen. Choose "fill" to let the game find teammates for you before the match starts.

You'll also need to master the game's controls. There is no room for mistakes when you're in the middle of a fast-paced battle!

If this all sounds overwhelming, don't worry. With the right knowledge and plenty of practice, you can become a *Fortnite* pro. Read on to start learning everything you need to know to master the game's thrilling combat.

Chapter 2

The Right Tools for the Job

At the start of each *Fortnite* match, you will land on an island with nothing but a pickaxe. This won't help you much in a fight. This means the first thing you'll need to do in any match is **scavenge** for weapons, ammo, and other important supplies.

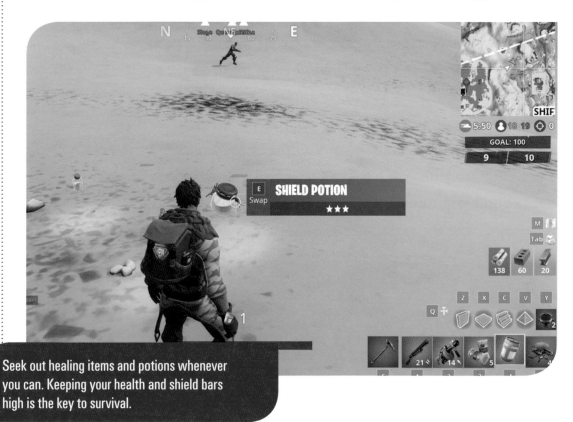

Seek out healing items and potions whenever you can. Keeping your health and shield bars high is the key to survival.

The Rift-to-Go item will instantly transport you back into the sky, allowing you to dive down to a new location on the map.

As you start scavenging, you might be amazed at the variety of things you can collect. There are grenades, healing items, and building materials. There are weird items like balloons that let you float up into the sky. But perhaps most importantly, there are many, many weapons. You will need to get to know all of them if you want to become a combat expert in *Fortnite*.

The weapons in *Fortnite* can be divided into several main categories: assault rifles, submachine guns (SMGs), pistols, machine guns, shotguns, sniper rifles, and explosive launchers. Each weapon handles a little differently. They fire at different rates and do different amounts of damage at different ranges.

Assault rifles, SMGs, and pistols are good all-around weapons that work best at medium range. Machine guns can do a lot of damage, but they are slow to start firing. This makes them perfect for destroying enemy forts, but not so good for a fast-paced fight. Shotguns work great at close range.

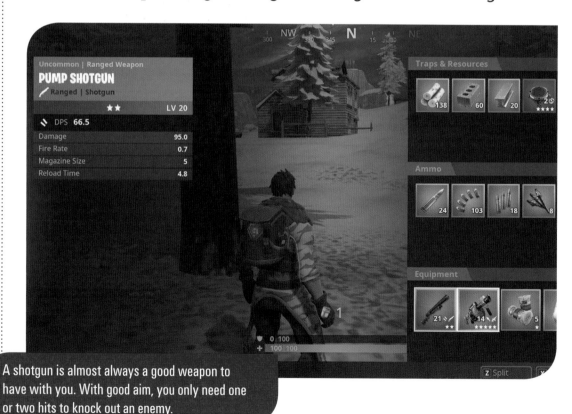

A shotgun is almost always a good weapon to have with you. With good aim, you only need one or two hits to knock out an enemy.

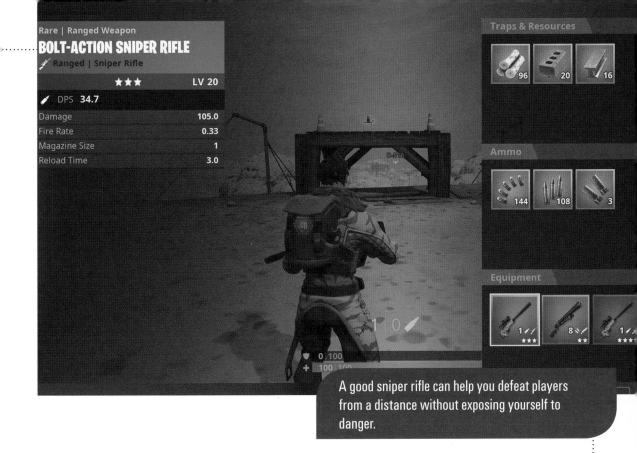

Rare | Ranged Weapon

BOLT-ACTION SNIPER RIFLE
Ranged | Sniper Rifle

★★★ LV 20

DPS **34.7**

Damage	105.0
Fire Rate	0.33
Magazine Size	1
Reload Time	3.0

Traps & Resources

96 20 16

Ammo

144 108 3

Equipment

A good sniper rifle can help you defeat players from a distance without exposing yourself to danger.

They do a lot of damage and you don't have to worry about perfect aim. Sniper rifles are great for attacking far-off enemies, but they are too slow to work in closer fights. Explosive launchers can fire grenades and rockets. They do a ton of damage and can travel long distances. However, they are very slow to fire.

Within each category, there are also different versions of each weapon. For example, you can find assault rifles that come with or without scopes. Semi-auto sniper rifles can reload faster than bolt-action sniper rifles. Experiment and try out all the

Customizing Your Controls

Do you ever wish that you could aim faster in *Fortnite*? Or that you could change which button on your controller causes your character to jump? You're in luck. The game will let you adjust many control settings. Simply access the Settings menu from the lobby, then access the control settings. You can make many different adjustments depending on which version of the game you are playing. For example, if you are playing the PC version, you can adjust the speed at which the game's view will change as you move your mouse. If you are playing the PlayStation 4 version, you can choose from different controller layouts.

If you ever find the game uncomfortable or difficult to control, try changing some of these settings. Play a little while and see if you like it more. You can always change it back if you don't like it. Every *Fortnite* player is different, and people have had success with many control styles. Find the one that suits you best!

different weapon types as you find them. This will give you a feel for which ones you like best.

Another thing to consider is a weapon's rarity. You have probably noticed that the weapons lying on the ground glow in different colors. These aren't just for show. Each color stands for a different level of rarity. Rarer weapons are more powerful than common ones. Here are what the different colors mean, in order from most common to rarest:

COLOR	RARITY
Gray	Common
Green	Uncommon
Blue	Rare
Purple	Epic
Orange/Gold	Legendary

If you are carrying a weapon of one type and you find a rarer version, pick it up! The difference in damage produced by weapons at different levels of rarity can be enough to turn a battle in your favor.

Each type of weapon has strengths and weaknesses. All of them can be of use in different situations. But none of them is the best choice for every situation. This means you'll need to find and carry multiple weapons if you want to succeed. For example, many players choose to carry a shotgun and a sniper rifle. This gives them a weapon that works well up close and one that works well at long distance.

No matter how good your weapons are, you won't have much luck if you don't have good aim. Practice firing different guns and trying to hit moving targets.

Your enemies will rarely stand still and let you take aim at them. You will need to be able to pinpoint them even while staying on the move yourself. The only way to get better at this is to practice!

One thing to remember while aiming is that your shots will take some time to reach distant enemies. This means you have to lead them. Instead of aiming a sniper shot right at an enemy, try to aim a little in front of the direction they are moving toward. The farther

When using scoped weapons, you always need to consider your target's distance while you aim.

away they are and the faster they are moving, the farther ahead you will need to aim.

Once you are really good at aiming, try to hit enemies in the body or head. These shots will do more damage than hitting an enemy's arms or legs. The best *Fortnite* players aim for head shots as often as they can. This gives them a smaller target, but they are rewarded big-time if they succeed. A single head shot from a powerful weapon can knock out an enemy in one hit!

Chapter 3

Joining the Fight

Once you feel comfortable using the many different weapons in *Fortnite*, you'll be ready to start working on your battle strategies. Charging headfirst into the thick of every fight isn't usually the best way to win at *Fortnite*. However, it is

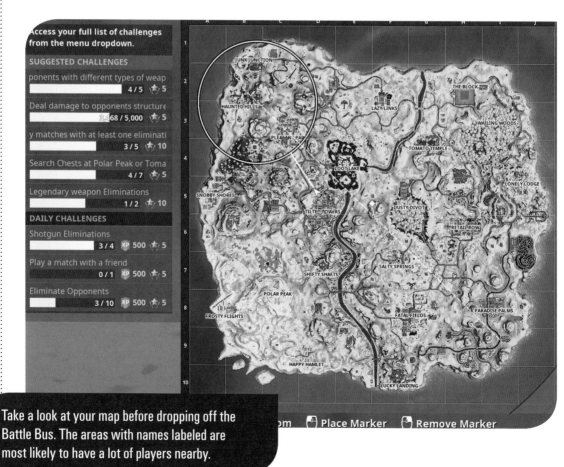

Take a look at your map before dropping off the Battle Bus. The areas with names labeled are most likely to have a lot of players nearby.

With its tall buildings and large amount of loot, Tilted Towers is usually one of the most popular spots for players to land.

the best way to practice your combat skills! At the start of a match, try parachuting near a popular area such as Tilted Towers. Here, there will almost always be plenty of rival players to fight against.

To practice fighting, you should be aggressive. But that doesn't mean you should blindly run toward every enemy with guns blazing. Instead, think carefully about each and every fight. What is the best way to approach your enemy? Which weapons should you use? Which strategies will give you an advantage?

The best situations are when you spot enemies before they see you. Before attacking, take a moment to observe your opponents. Stay hidden and watch them. What are they doing? Have they noticed you? Do they seem to have powerful weapons? These things can all affect the fight ahead, so pay close attention.

One of the most important things to consider when fighting in *Fortnite* is which direction to attack from. Obviously, you should try to approach enemies from

If you are playing with teammates, open your map and click anywhere to set a beacon. Your teammates will be able to see it as a glowing light. This tells them where you want them to go.

Use Your Ears

You might want to listen to music or chat with friends as you play *Fortnite*. But if you want to win, you will need to keep your ears focused on the game's sound effects. In *Fortnite*, you will often hear nearby enemies before you can see them. Almost everything you do in the game creates noise. Running creates the sound of footsteps. Gunshots make a lot of noise. Chopping down a tree makes a certain sound. If you have good speakers or you are wearing headphones, you can even hear which direction these sounds are coming from. This can give you a huge advantage in surprising enemies or avoiding danger.

Keep in mind that other players can hear you just as easily as you can hear them. Don't fire your weapons unless you are in a fight. You might alert enemies to your location. If you need to knock walls down to get building materials, make sure there are no rival players nearby before you start.

behind or from the side to avoid being seen. But you should also think vertically. Getting the high ground offers a huge advantage in any *Fortnite* battle. This is one reason you will often see great players quickly trying to build tall towers when fighting opponents. You can also take the high ground from atop a hill or cliff or by standing on one of the premade buildings scattered across the *Fortnite* island.

There are many good reasons to attack from above whenever you can. First, being up high will allow you to easily see everything that is going on below you. You will be able to see which direction your opponents are running in, no matter which way they go. You will also have a better chance of seeing players that try to sneak up on you. Your enemies below, on the other hand, will have a harder time keeping track of your movements. The structure you are standing on will partially block their view.

When you are above opponents, your attacks will also have a better chance of hitting them in the head. As you learned in the previous chapter, this does a great deal of damage. At the same time, your enemies will have a very difficult time hitting your character in the head. Their shots will more likely hit your character in the feet, if they connect at all.

Of course, you will not always be so lucky as to have the high ground in every fight. So what do you do when your opponent has a height advantage over you? This can be a very tricky situation. Staying on the ground is no good. If you start building ramps to climb toward them, they will likely be able to defeat you before you get close enough. One possibility is to build your own tower some distance away from the

A quickly built ramp allows you to see your surroundings better while also providing some cover.

enemy. If you are a fast enough builder, you might be able to get a height advantage of your own.

Don't be afraid to flee if you get into a fight you can't win. Be sure to build defensively as you run away. Use walls to give yourself cover and make it harder for your enemy to see which way you're heading. Once you are in a safe location, decide if you want to continue the fight or keep running. You might find that you've confused your enemy. Now you can surprise with a counterattack!

No matter what you're doing, you should almost always be on the move in *Fortnite*. In some games, it is a good strategy to hide and attack enemies from one well-defended location. This does not work well in *Fortnite*. If you stand still, your enemies will use walls and other structures to box you in. You will then be an easy target. Also, don't forget that the storm circle is

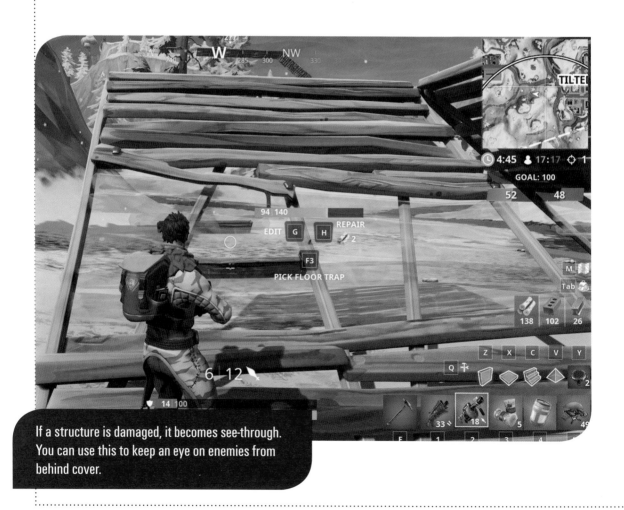

If a structure is damaged, it becomes see-through. You can use this to keep an eye on enemies from behind cover.

always shrinking. You don't want to be caught outside it when this happens.

You will likely spot other players fighting in the distance from time to time. When this happens, stay out of sight and watch the fight. Eventually one player will win. But he or she will likely be damaged and not ready for another fight yet. This is a great time to launch an attack of your own and catch your opponent off guard. You will get to pick up the dropped gear from the player you defeat as well as from the player your opponent defeated while you watched.

Chapter 4

Don't Give Up!

Fighting in *Fortnite* can be a lot of fun. But when you find yourself facing off against a seemingly endless wave of great players, it can also be frustrating. Maybe you know exactly what strategy you should use, but you just don't have the fastest reflexes. Or maybe you are just having bad luck scavenging for good weapons. Don't give up in these situations.

You will probably need to practice a lot before you are able to win your first Victory Royale.

Don't keep staring in the same direction as you move. Turn around and look from side to side as often as you can.

Not every match will go your way. There is some luck involved in *Fortnite*. But if you keep practicing, you will find yourself winning more and more fights.

Always remember that there are many players in a *Fortnite* match. Unless you are one of just a couple of players remaining, avoid focusing too much on any one opponent. If you are not paying attention, other players could sneak up on you while you are distracted. Just as you can observe your enemies from a distance, they can do the same to you. Be ready for a fight at any time!

One of the best ways to get better and learn new skills in *Fortnite* is to watch experienced players in action. Many of the top players in the world stream their games regularly on services such as YouTube and Twitch. Watching them is fun and entertaining, but it can also help you get better at the game. Pay close attention to the way the pros play. Which strategies do they use in different situations? Which weapons do

Watching other players in action is a great way to see what you're doing wrong and look for ways to improve.

Keep Your Cool

No matter how good you get at combat, you won't win every fight in *Fortnite*. There might even be times when you keep getting defeated over and over again. This can naturally lead you to get upset. But no matter how badly things seem to be going, you should always try to stay relaxed when you play. Getting angry and tense will only cause you to start making more mistakes. It also just isn't a very fun way to play!

If you notice yourself getting frustrated or mad, try taking a little break from *Fortnite*. The next time you play, you'll be back at the top of your game. When you are calm, you will make better choices. Your reflexes and aim will improve. You'll soon be winning plenty of battles again.

they prefer? You might be able to pick up a few tricks and practice them yourself.

The most important thing to do if you want to be good at *Fortnite* combat is to just keep playing. Remember that there is no penalty for losing a match. You can try over and over again as much as you like. Each time a match ends, you can be playing again just a few seconds later. Try crazy new things. Don't be afraid to attack really good players. Get out there and practice aiming, building, and moving. Fighting in *Fortnite* will start to feel as natural as riding a bike. It won't be long before you claim first place as the last player standing!

Glossary

revive (rih-VIYV) to bring back to life

scavenge (SKAV-uhnj) to search for useful items

streamers (STREE-murz) people who broadcast themselves playing video games and talking online

Find Out More

BOOKS

Cunningham, Kevin. *Video Game Designer*. Ann Arbor, MI: Cherry Lake Publishing, 2016.

Powell, Marie. *Asking Questions About Video Games*. Ann Arbor, MI: Cherry Lake Publishing, 2016.

WEBSITES

Epic Games—Fortnite

www.epicgames.com/fortnite/en-US/home
Check out the official *Fortnite* website.

Fortnite Wiki

https://fortnite.gamepedia.com/Fortnite_Wiki
This fan-made website offers up-to-date information on the latest additions to *Fortnite*.

Index

About the Author

Josh Gregory is the author of more than 125 books for kids. He has written about everything from animals to technology to history. A graduate of the University of Missouri–Columbia, he currently lives in Chicago, Illinois.